NFL

NATIONAL FOOTBALL LEAGUE
PLAYMAKERS
READER

by Tim Polzer

SCHOLASTIC INC.

New York   Toronto   London   Auckland   Sydney

Mexico City   New Delhi   Hong Kong   Buenos Aires

ISBN: 0-439-84838-5

Published by Scholastic Inc.
SCHOLASTIC and associated logos are trademarks and/or registered
trademarks of Scholastic Inc.

12 11 10 9 8 7 6 5 4 3 2 1   6 7 8 9 10/0

Designed by Kim Brown
Printed in the U.S.A.
Printing, August 2006

TABLE OF CONTENTS

TIKI BARBER

At 5'10", 200 pounds, Tiki Barber may be considered small when compared to most NFL running backs, but he truly plays like a giant in a New York uniform. He is perhaps the team's most popular player and is known for flashing his smile and always having a lot to say to his teammates, fans, and the media.

While many NFL running backs lose a step of speed and quickness as they grow older, this veteran only gets better. Tiki produced a career season in 2005, rushing for 1,860 yards for an average of 5.2 yards per carry. He finished just a few yards behind Seattle Seahawk Shaun Alexander for the NFL rushing title. Tiki also scored nine touchdowns on the ground. Tiki's abilities as a receiver make him even more valuable to the Giants' offense. He caught 54 passes for 530 yards and two touchdowns in 2005.

Tiki's offensive production was historic. His combined 2,390 all-purpose yards were the most by an NFL player over the age of 30 and second only to Marshall Faulk's NFL record 2,429 total yards in 1999.

Tiki's success was the result of more than just being a smart veteran player. It was the product of a lot of hard work and determination since his rookie season. Things didn't always go so well early in Tiki's NFL career. As a young player, he had a problem holding on to the football. He fumbled the ball at least eight times in four consecutive seasons before he found a cure. Tiki adjusted the position in which he carried the ball when he was running and focused on protecting the ball at all times. The change helped Tiki limit his fumbles to just one in 2005.

On December 17, 2005, Tiki made New York Giants history. Tiki broke the Giants' single-game rushing record with 220 yards against the Kansas City Chiefs. Afterward, Tiki said he had promised and dedicated his record-breaking performance to team owner Wellington Mara, who passed away on October 25, 2005. The Giants' owner was an important person in Tiki's life, beginning with his rookie season of 1997.

NFL running backs rarely run for more than 200 yards in a game, but Tiki topped the mark three times that season. He also took off on a 95-yard touchdown run against the Oakland Raiders that was the longest in Giants history. The team's previous record—Hap Moran's 91-yard run in 1930—was more than 75 seasons old.

The Giants drafted Tiki in the second round of the 1997 NFL Draft after he became the first player to rush for 1,000 yards in back-to-back seasons at the University of Virginia. While most NFL players attend college on an athletic scholarship, Tiki's grades were so good in high school, he was awarded an academic scholarship. He also was a part of the Cavaliers' track team as a long jumper and a member of their relay team.

Tiki particularly enjoyed playing on the same college team with his brother, Ronde. Tiki and Ronde are one of the few sets of identical twins ever to play in the NFL. Ronde, who plays defensive back for the Tampa Bay Buccaneers, has been voted to the Pro Bowl, just like his brother.

While both Barber twins have played in the Super Bowl, Ronde is the only brother who has won a league championship. The brothers are competitive, but they do not let the fact that they play on competing teams get in the way of their relationship. They have appeared together in television commercials and also wrote a children's book. The book tells the story of a young football player learning the importance of teamwork. It's a lesson that both of the Barbers learned at an early age.

MATT HASSELBECK

The Seattle Seahawks' Matt Hasselbeck is one of the NFL's most determined quarterbacks, having worked his way from the practice squad to the Super Bowl. His love for hard work and football runs in the family.

Matt was only eight years old when his father, Don, played in a Super Bowl. In 1984, Matt sat in the stands of Tampa Stadium, watching his father's Los Angeles Raiders beat the Washington Redskins in Super Bowl XVIII. Matt's younger brother, Tim, also has played in the NFL as a quarterback.

In 2006, Matt realized his dream of playing in Super Bowl XL, but came away disappointed when his team lost to the Pittsburgh

Steelers, 21–10. He left the championship game even more resolved to improve and return to the Super Bowl.

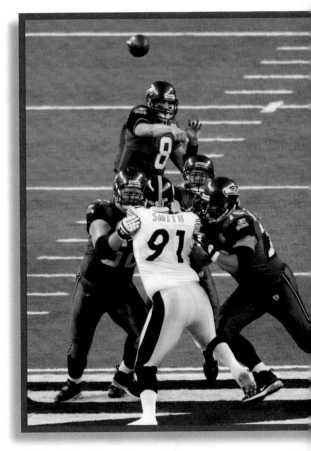

In leading the Seahawks to their first Super Bowl appearance in team history, Matt proved himself to be one of the NFL's most accurate passers. He completed an amazing 65.5 percent of his passes for 3,459 yards and 24 touchdowns. The performance earned him his second trip to the Pro Bowl.

In the divisional round of the 2005 playoffs, Matt was faced with an unexpected and difficult challenge. When running back Shaun Alexander—the league's Most Valuable Player—was injured early in the first quarter against Washington, Matt had to take over the Seahawks' offense. He stepped forward as a leader who would not let the team get down. He guided the Seahawks to a halftime lead with a 29-yard touchdown pass to Darrell Jackson and later scored the game-winning touchdown on a six-yard run against one of the NFL's toughest defenses.

Matt has become a successful professional quarterback, but his NFL career started slowly. After playing at Boston College, he was drafted by the Green Bay Packers in the sixth round of the 1998 NFL Draft. As a rookie, Matt never got to suit up for a game. He spent the entire season on the Packers' practice squad, trying to learn the team's West Coast offense under head coach Mike Holmgren, who, before coming to Green Bay, tutored Pro Football Hall of Fame quarterback Joe Montana as the offensive coordinator of the San Francisco 49ers. Joe won four Super Bowls during his seasons in San Francisco.

Matt was a quick learner, proving it one season later, when he earned the team's backup role behind another NFL quarterback legend, Brett Favre. He studied behind Favre for three seasons, but did not lose his patience. With a superstar like Brett ahead of him, Matt did not get to play many downs during the regular season. He did contribute as the team's holder on extra points and field goals—and even threw a touchdown pass off a fake field-goal attempt.

Matt also used his time as Brett's backup to learn from one of the NFL's best quarterbacks. Matt said the most important thing Brett taught him was to have no fear.

When Coach Holmgren left Green Bay to become the Seahawks' head coach and general manager, he traded for Matt. Coach Holmgren believed that Matt could develop into the Seahawks' starting quarterback of the future.

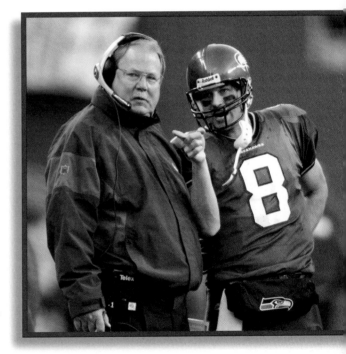

The future came quickly for Matt, who opened his first season with the Seahawks as the team's starting quarterback. He started 12 games in 2001, but unfortunately was limited by injuries.

The following year, Matt entered the Seahawks' training camp as the backup behind quarterback Trent Dilfer, but soon he was promoted to starter. He passed for more than 300 yards in four games and even threw for more than 400 yards twice. His completion percentage of 63.7 was the best in the National Football Conference.

Matt turned into one of the NFL's best quarterbacks in his third year in Seattle. He became the Seahawks' all-time highest-rated passer, passed for a team record 3,841 yards, and earned a trip to the Pro Bowl. He even led the Seahawks to their first playoff trip in four years.

Matt's confidence in his abilities and in his team were show-cased when he returned to Green Bay to face Favre and the Packers in a playoff game. After leading the Seahawks to a last-second touchdown that tied the score, Matt walked to the center of the field to call the coin toss prior to overtime. When the referee asked him if the Seahawks would kick or receive, Matt said: "We want the ball, and we're going to score."

Unfortunately, one of Matt's receivers ran the wrong route, leading to an interception that cost the Seahawks the game. Matt never discussed his receiver's mistake with the media. He knew that one player does not lose a game for an entire team—and that a good teammate would not complain or point fingers. He just decided to work even harder.

BEN ROETHLISBERGER

A funny thing happened on Ben Roethlisberger's way to the Super Bowl. In addition to throwing two touchdown passes, the Pittsburgh Steelers quarterback also made a game-saving tackle that allowed his team to advance one step closer to their first

Super Bowl in ten seasons. It was a strange accomplishment for one of the NFL's most promising quarterbacks.

As Steelers running back Jerome Bettis was trying to score a late touchdown that would clinch a divisional playoff win against the Indianapolis Colts, he fumbled the football. A Colts defensive back picked up the loose ball and began sprinting toward the Steelers' end zone. Ben somehow managed to slow the Colt player down and trip him up, preventing a touchdown that would have given Indianapolis a last-minute victory.

One week later, Ben left the tackling to the Pittsburgh defense and used his passing arm to help the Steelers in the American Football Conference Championship game. Against the Denver Broncos, he completed 21 of 29 passes for 275 yards and two touchdowns. He even scored a rushing touchdown to lead the Steelers to the win—and to a showdown with the Seattle Seahawks in Super Bowl XL.

At 6'5", Ben is one of the tallest starting quarterbacks in the NFL. His fans have nicknamed him "Big Ben" for his height and ability to stand tall in the pocket and keep his cool under pressure. His height—Peyton Manning, Carson Palmer, and Byron Leftwich are just as tall—helps Ben see over onrushing defensive linemen and spy blitzes designed to hurry his passes.

These talents, along with Ben's strong work ethic and determination, helped the 23-year-old overcome any nervousness as
the second youngest quarterback—after Dan Marino—to ever
start a Super Bowl. Ben and the Steelers beat the Seahawks and
earned his Super Bowl ring in just his second NFL season.

NFL success came surprisingly early for Ben, who enjoyed a
dream season as a rookie. The Steelers chose Ben with the elev-
enth overall pick in the 2004 NFL Draft. He was a highly rated
quarterback prospect from Miami University in Ohio, where he
set almost every major passing record, even though he played
only three seasons.

It wasn't long before Ben was forced into action when the
Steelers starting quarterback, Tommy Maddox, was injured in the

second game of the season. Wearing number seven in honor of his hero, former Denver Broncos quarterback John Elway, Ben trotted onto the field against Baltimore and had his second pass attempt intercepted by the Ravens. Instead of getting down on himself, Ben went back on the field and threw two touchdown passes in his first NFL action.

From then on, Ben made the best of his opportunity, showing strong leadership and an understanding of the Steelers' offense, while limiting his mistakes. He led the Steelers to 13 wins without a loss in his first regular season. He later set an NFL record with 15 consecutive wins before suffering his first loss as a starting quarterback. Along the way, Ben also set several rookie passing records, including highest passer rating (98.1) and completion percentage (66.4).

He even helped the Steelers defeat the New England Patriots, ending the then-Super Bowl champions 21-game winning streak. Unfortunately for the Steelers, Ben's rookie season ended one game short of the Super Bowl when the Patriots later defeated the Steelers in the AFC Championship game.

Ben used his disappointment to fuel his work for the future. He asked veteran Jerome Bettis to hold off his plans to retire. Ben promised Jerome, whose nickname is "The Bus," that he would lead the team back to the Super Bowl. It turned out to be a promise Ben would keep.

STEVE SMITH

Steve Smith, one of the NFL's fastest players, had to over-come a major injury on his way to becoming one of the league's most exciting and versatile game breakers.

The Carolina Panthers' 5'9", 185-pound receiver is one of the NFL's quickest and most elusive playmakers. His ability to turn a short pass into a long touchdown is feared by his NFL opponents. He's also one of the best punt and kick returners in professional football.

Steve was voted to the Pro Bowl after the 2005 season and was named co-winner of the NFL's Comeback Player of the Year Award. He earned the honor after fighting his way back from a serious leg injury to lead the NFL with 1,563 yards and tying for the league's best with 103 receptions and 12 touchdowns. The versatile performer also became the only NFL player to gain 1,900 or more total yards in each of his first three seasons.

The Panthers drafted Steve in the third round of the 2001 NFL Draft. He started his college career at Santa Monica College in California before transferring to the University of Utah, where Steve set the school record by averaging 20.6 yards per catch.

Steve caught the attention of NFL scouts by returning a kickoff for a touchdown in the 2000 Blue–Gray game. His special-teams skills made him even more valuable as a player.

In his first pro season, Steve saw most of his playing time on special teams, leading all rookies with 1,994 net yards, fourth behind only Priest Holmes, Marshall Faulk, and Derrick Mason. As a result, Steve was the only rookie selected for the Pro Bowl.

By his second NFL season, Steve had earned a chance to start at wide receiver. Steve showed that he was worthy of the promotion, with 54 receptions for 872 yards and three touchdowns. A year later, he blossomed into a top-notch receiver, catching 88 passes for 1,110 yards and seven touchdowns.

Steve also continued to perform as one of the NFL's best return men. Against the Cincinnati Bengals, he became the second NFL player to return two punts for touchdowns and catch a touchdown pass in the same game.

The Panthers were the surprise winners of the NFC South division and shocked the NFL by fighting their way through the playoffs toward their first Super Bowl. The team earned the nickname "Cardiac Cats" for their habit of winning games in the final minutes.

It was during the postseason that Steve really made a name for himself. In the Panthers' divisional playoff game against the St. Louis Rams, Steve caught a 69-yard, game-winning touchdown pass in double overtime—the longest play ever to end an NFL postseason game.

Steve and the Panthers next traveled to Philadelphia, where

they upset the heavily favored Eagles in the NFC Championship game. Steve wound up leading the NFL in the 2003 postseason with three touchdowns and 18 catches for 404 receiving yards, the most by a player during the postseason since former San Francisco 49ers superstar Jerry Rice totaled 204 yards in 1988.

In Super Bowl XXXVIII, Steve continued his postseason hot streak by scoring the Panthers' first touchdown of the championship game on a 39-yard pass from quarterback Jake Delhomme.

Unfortunately for Steve, the Patriots kicked a last-minute field goal to win the Super Bowl, but the receiver and his Panthers teammates were determined to work hard and win a Super Bowl as soon as possible.

The following year, Steve and the Panthers were considered among the teams favored to return to the Super Bowl, but Steve suffered a broken leg in the first game of the season. He turned out to be one of 14 Panthers players to be listed on the team's injured reserve list that season.

Steve used his time away from the field to concentrate on his recovery and become an even better receiver. That hard work paid off when he turned in another strong postseason that included 27 receptions for 335 yards and three touchdowns. It was an amazing performance that caused Dallas Cowboys coach Bill Parcells to call Steve the best player in the league.

BRIAN URLACHER

Brian Urlacher has earned his reputation as the latest in a long line of big-hitting middle linebackers who played for the Chicago Bears. At 6'4", 258 pounds, he's a big player who is surprisingly fast for his size. He uses his combination of strength and quickness to track down—and tackle—opposing ball carriers.

In 2005, Brian, whose number 54 replica jersey is among the league's bestselling items, made 121 tackles and six quarterback sacks on his way to being voted the NFL's Defensive Player of the Year.

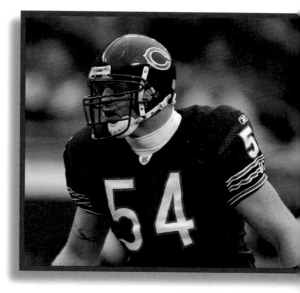

The Bears have a long history of great middle linebackers. Their fans enjoy hard-hitting, physical football players and strong defenses. The team lives up to Chicago's nickname "City of the Big Shoulders." The Bears have certainly suited up their share of linebackers with big shoulders. Dick Butkus and Mike Singletary were both selected to the Pro Football Hall of Fame after leading the Bears' defense. Dick was the Bears' first draft pick in 1965. He was elected to eight straight Pro Bowls before retiring in 1973. Mike, who was known for his wide, intense eyes, played for the Bears from 1981 to 1992 and was voted to ten consecutive Pro Bowls. Mike was the leader of a Bears defensive unit that earned a reputation as one of the best in NFL history—and also earned a victory over the New England Patriots in Super Bowl XX.

After Mike retired, the Bears looked long and hard for a middle linebacker who could be a cornerstone and return the Chicago defense to glory. The Bears found their man in New Mexico in 2000.

Strangely, Brian was not playing linebacker when the Bears first noticed him. He played strong safety in high school and at the University of New Mexico. As a New Mexico Lobo, he was so fast, his coach even let him return kicks and punts. He also caught six touchdown passes as a part-time receiver. He amassed 442 tackles, 11 sacks, and three interceptions in just two seasons in New Mexico.

Even though Brian was a safety, the Bears thought he possessed a special combination of size, speed, and aggressiveness.

After all, he was an All-America selection and winner of the Jim
Thorpe Award as the nation's outstanding college defensive back.
The team also believed that Brian was ferocious enough to fight
off opposing blockers in the middle.

The Bears selected Brian ninth overall in the 2000 NFL Draft
with hopes that he would be their next legendary middle linebacker. Neither the team nor the city could wait to watch Brian
play in a Bears uniform. As it turns out, they had to wait a few
games.

Believing that immediately shifting Brian to middle linebacker
would be too much for him to learn too quickly, the Bears put
him at strong-side linebacker to start the season. Brian struggled

with the new position, until the team finally let him play middle linebacker in the third game of his rookie season. His struggles were over as he made 13 tackles and his first NFL sack in his debut in the middle.

After recording 124 tackles, eight sacks, and two interceptions his first season, Brian was named the NFL's Defensive Rookie of the Year and voted an alternate for the Pro Bowl.

In his second season, Brian continued his dominance on defense and also scored two touchdowns. He returned a fumble 90 yards for one touchdown and was on the receiving end of a pass on a fake field-goal attempt that turned into the game-winning score.

He also earned his place among the Bears' all-time great linebackers. According to Bears statistics, Brian made a record 214 tackles in 2002, besting Dick Butkus's previous team record. He also became the first Bears player since Mike Singletary to lead the team in tackles for four straight years.

ROY WILLIAMS

Running backs and receivers fear running across the middle when Dallas Cowboy safety Roy Williams is patrolling the field. Williams is one of the NFL's hardest-hitting defensive backs and is known for causing fumbles and chaos among opposing offenses.

At 6'0", 226 pounds, Roy is one of the biggest safeties in the league—almost big enough to be a linebacker—and he uses his size to his advantage. Roy is at his best when the Cowboys' defensive scheme allows him to position himself close to the line of scrimmage where he can provide support against the run or blitz the passer. When opposing quarterbacks approach the line, they always look to see where Roy lines up so they can warn their blockers that he's coming.

The Cowboys first noticed Roy's habit for making big plays when he was at the University of Oklahoma. In a game against archrival Texas, Roy made an unforgettable play, leaping over the Longhorns' offensive linemen to grab the Texas quarterback and cause an interception that was returned for a Sooners touchdown. It was the type of athletic play most safeties can only dream of making.

With plays like that on his highlight reel, it is no surprise that Roy was one of the best defensive players in Oklahoma history. He was named the winner of the Bronko Nagurski Award as the nation's top defender. And, just like Brian Urlacher, Roy also won the Jim Thorpe Award as the nation's top defensive back.

More important, Roy was a leader on the undefeated 2000 Oklahoma team that won a national championship. With a successful college career behind him, NFL scouts realized, Roy was a player who knew how to hit and knew how to win.

The Cowboys did not hesitate to use their first-round draft pick on Roy with the eighth overall selection of the 2002 NFL Draft. And it did not take long for him to convince his new team that they had made the right choice. He instantly became a starter in his first training camp—the first Cowboys rookie to start at safety in 15 years—and has maintained his strong hold on the position ever since.

Roy quickly built a reputation for always being around the ball, grabbing five interceptions as a rookie and returning two for touchdowns. He also recorded seven tackles for lost yardage and forced three fumbles, while recovering two turnovers. The performance was good enough to earn All-Rookie honors.

Roy has been selected to three Pro Bowls since his rookie season. In the 2006 all-star game, Roy intercepted a Peyton Manning pass and lateraled the ball back to Falcons cornerback DeAngelo Hall, who returned it 57 yards to set up an NFC touchdown.

Roy also consistently ranks among the Cowboys' leaders in tackles and promises to be one of the Cowboys' defensive leaders for seasons to come.

While Roy may unleash some scary hard hits when he's on the field, he's a nice guy off the field. Roy is an active supporter of many charities and youth sports programs. He heads the Roy Williams Safety Net Foundation, a program that provides assistance, resources, and suppo to mothers struggling to raise their children.